First published in the United States by Silver Burdett Press, 1989

English adaptation © 1989 Silver Burdett Press

Collection dirigée par Martine et Daniel Sassier

© 1988 by Editions des Deux Coqs d'Or, Paris

Library of Congress Cataloging-in-Publication Data

Poth, Cathy.
    Earth/English text, Cathy Poth.
      p.   cm.—(Look & learn)
    Adaptation of: La terre / Pierre Avérous.
    Includes index.
    Summary: An introduction to the earth, its crust, water, air, animals, and moon.
    1. Earth—Juvenile literature.   [1. Earth]
I. Avérous, Pierre, 1946-   . Terre. II. Title.
III. Series: Poth, Cathy. Look & learn.
QB637.4.P68 1989   551   89-6273
ISBN 0-382-09826-9 (lib. bdg.)
ISBN 0-382-09827-7 (pbk.)

The Earth

Illustrations by Monique Gorde
Adapted by Cathy Poth from an
original French text by Pierre Avérous

Silver Burdett Press
Englewood Cliffs, New Jersey

Table of Contents

THE EARTH: AN ENORMOUS

A Special Balloon

The earth we live on is round, like this balloon. But a balloon is full of air. It floats wherever the wind carries it. The earth is solid. It always moves through space in the same way, as if it were stuck on an **invisible** track. Of course, the earth is also much larger than a balloon. Suppose you wanted to walk around the earth. If you started today, you wouldn't finish your trip for at least four years!

Round Earth

This ladybug is walking on a round lamp shade. In the same way, people walk on the round earth. But, because the earth is so big, we can't see that it is round. Suppose you decide to walk from one end of town to another. This seems far, doesn't it? You are still only traveling across a very small part of the enormous earth. Long ago everyone thought the earth was flat. This is because the small part that can be seen looks flat.

Wrinkles and Bumps All Over

The **surface** of the earth is not smooth like a ball. Like the wrinkles and bumps on this bed, the earth has many hills and valleys. Just look around and you will see them. Besides hills and valleys, there are **plains** and very high mountains. If you fly in an airplane, look down at the earth. You will see that the earth is very bumpy.

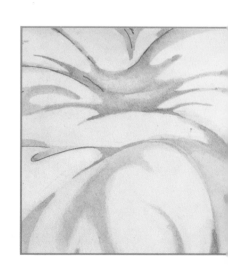

BALLOON

Continents and Oceans

This is a picture of a **globe**. A globe is a round model that shows what the earth looks like. On the earth, there are **continents**. Continents are very large areas of land. On a globe the continents are shown in yellow and green. The blue areas on the globe are the oceans. Look at a globe. You will see that most of the earth is covered with water.

Inside the Earth

The earth is not full of air like a balloon. The inside of the earth is rock. Some of this rock is very, very hot. Suppose we could cut the earth in half. We would see the different kinds of rock that make up the earth. Scientists have tried to study this rock. But it is very hard to dig deep enough. The earth is wrapped in a thin skin, like an apple. All we can see on the earth is this thin skin.

Giant Satellites

In some ways a **satellite** is like the earth. A satellite moves through space like the earth. Both satellites and the earth stay in space without string, wings, or a motor. Satellites are put in space by rockets. They take pictures of the earth. They also help us send messages from one part of the earth to another.

Years ago people thought the earth was flat. They believed if you sailed too far into the ocean you would fall off the end of the world!

Monique Gorde

THE MOVING EARTH

A Giant Spinning Top

The earth is always spinning, just like a top. It takes twenty-four hours for the earth to turn around, or **rotate**, once. Twenty-four hours equals one day. So it takes one day for the earth to rotate once. As the earth spins, different parts of the earth face the sun. During the day we are facing the sun. At night we have rotated away from it. This is why in daytime it is light and at nighttime it is dark.

Turning with the Earth

When you ride on a merry-go-round, sometimes it feels like you are standing still. Everything around you looks like it is spinning. Actually, you are moving as the merry-go-round turns. Everything around you is standing still. On earth it is the same. We are turning with the rotating earth. But we cannot feel that we are moving.

Day and Night

The light on the earth comes from the sun. As it shines, we can see everything around us. Have you ever seen the sun rise in the morning and set in the evening? Did you notice that the sun seemed to be moving? As the earth turns, it looks like the sun is moving across the sky. But it is the earth that is moving while the sun stays still. As the earth turns without stopping, so days and nights follow each other without stopping.

Shadows Grow and Shrink

When light from the sun strikes an object, the object makes a shadow on the ground. You, too, can make shadows when the sun is on your body. At noon, the sun is highest in the sky. Then our shadows are very small. In the morning and evening, our shadows grow very long. This is because the sun is low in the sky. Throughout the day, our shadows grow and shrink as the earth turns. Look at the shadows in the picture. Guess what time of day it is.

Cold Countries and Hot Countries

Countries in the middle of the earth get a lot of heat from the sun. These countries are hot all year round. There is never any snow in winter. Near the top and the bottom of the earth, the sun gives very little heat. In these parts of the earth, it is cold all year round. People must always wear heavy clothes to keep warm. Can you name any countries or states that are always hot? Can you name any that are always cold?

Moving Around the Sun

These children are sitting in little baskets that turn around the center of the big wheel. The earth turns around the sun in the same way. While the earth rotates, it also **revolves** around the sun. It takes a whole year to go around once—one spring, summer, fall, and winter. In summer the earth is tilted toward the sun. Then the rays are more concentrated and hotter. In winter the earth is tilted away from the sun. Then the suns rays are spread out and less hot.

Clouds move through the sky, too. They move because the wind is blowing them.

Monique Gorde

THE EARTH'S CRUST

Bending, Folding, and Shaping

The dough for this cake bends and folds as the baker shapes it. In some ways this is like the **crust**, or skin, that covers the earth. When we stand on the ground, the earth's crust feels very solid. Actually, the crust of the earth is bending and folding all the time. But it changes so slowly that we can't see it change. Mountains and some valleys are made by the moving crust of the earth. But most valleys are made by the wearing away of the land by rivers.

The Wind and Rain Move Things

This girl is pouring cream on the cake. The cream has washed away some of the cake's decorations. In this way, rain and rivers can wash away things from the land. Mud and plants often are washed from one part of the land to another. The wind, too, carries things as it blows. It can lift seeds from trees and other plants and carry them to other places. In ways like this the earth is always changing. What else does the wind carry when it blows?

Thick Layers of Dust and Dirt

Like the sugar sprinkles on this cake, little pieces of dust and dirt are carried by the wind. The wind drops them in cracks and holes in the earth's crust. Some dust blows out to sea and settles on the ocean floor. All over the earth dust and dirt are always moving. This happens year after year. Slowly this changes the way the earth looks.

A Volcano

It is so hot under the crust of the earth that rocks may melt. Sometimes this **liquid** rock shoots out of holes in the earth's crust. This huge explosion of hot air and melted rock builds a hill called a **volcano**. The hot liquid rock that comes out of the ground is called **lava**. Volcanoes are another way that the crust of the earth changes its shape.

Big Pieces of Ice

These little desserts are floating in cream. This is similar to what happens on the earth. In some very cold places, huge pieces of ice float in the sea or move on mountainsides. Some of these pieces are as big as islands. Those that float in the sea are called **icebergs**. Those that form on land are called **glaciers**. They change the surface of the land as they slowly move across it.

When the Earth's Crust Cracks

There are deep cracks in the crust of this bread. Sometimes the crust of the earth has cracks, too. These form when part of the earth shakes and moves very suddenly. This shaking and cracking of the earth's crust is called an **earthquake**. Can you guess what happens to tall buildings during an earthquake?

Volcanoes can be very dangerous. Their hot air can kill people before the lava even reaches them.

Everything Weighs Something

A basket full of apples is very heavy. It is hard to carry. The earth itself pulls everything down to the ground. Everything you pick up weighs something. Because the earth holds everything near to its surface, lots of things feel heavy.

Dropping Apples

It is fall. Apples are ripe in the orchards. If no one picks them, they will drop off the branches by themselves. **Gravity** is the force that pulls everything on the earth to the ground. It is gravity that keeps everything on the earth from floating away into space. Gravity pulls things to the earth as if they were attached by a long invisible elastic band.

Gravity and You

You, too, are held on the ground by gravity. Because of gravity, you will never float off into space. Gravity pulls everything on the earth to the ground. It keeps things in place. You can test gravity. Jump as high as you can. How long can you stay in the air? One second? Two seconds? Gravity is so strong that it quickly pulls you back to the ground.

EVERYTHING

Wings Take You Away

When you throw a ball into the air, it falls back to the earth. This is because of the earth's gravity. The birds in the picture are flying. To leave the ground and stay in the air, they must work against gravity. They do this by flapping their wings. Airplanes do this by using their engines. If they don't, gravity will pull them back down to the earth.

The Other Side of the Earth

Have you ever thought about people who live on the other side of the earth? Do they live upside down? Do they walk upside down? The answer is no. They walk just like you do, with their feet on the ground. This is because of the earth's gravity. It pulls everything to the center of the earth no matter where on the earth the object is. On the round earth, gravity pulls your feet to the ground. So no matter where you are, you're right side up.

The Earth and the Moon

The moon looks small from the earth because it is very far away. Even though the moon is very far away, the earth's gravity holds on to it out in space. The moon revolves around the earth just as the earth revolves around the sun. Sometimes you can see the moon even in daytime. But sometimes you can't see it, even at night. This is because it is on the other side of the earth.

It is easy for butterflies to fly away from the earth's gravity. Why do you think this is so?

THE EARTH IS FULL OF WATER

Water Moves Down

The earth's gravity holds on to water, too. Water is kept close to the earth just like everything else is. Rivers and rainwater high on a mountain will always **flow** down to the lowest ground. This is the work of gravity. Rain falls from the sky because of gravity. Water from a faucet and rain on a roof all flow down toward the ground.

Lakes Are Big Puddles

When water in a river flows down a mountain, it stops at the lowest point below the mountain. There the water forms a big puddle. The puddle gets bigger and bigger. Finally it becomes a large lake. Often a lake forms where there is already a big hole in the earth's crust. This makes an easy place for the water to settle. Very big holes in the earth's crust that are filled with water are the seas and the oceans.

Rain

When the sun heats the oceans and rivers of the earth, tiny particles of water rise into the air. This is called **evaporation**. At first, these drops of water are so small and light that we cannot see them. But soon the drops become a group of drops, and this makes a cloud. Eventually, the cloud gets so full of drops that it can't hold any more. The drops then fall from the cloud to the earth. This is what we call rain!

Like a Sponge

After it has rained, most of the rain evaporates back into the sky. Or it flows into rivers and lakes. But there is always some water that sinks into the earth. This water keeps the ground a little wet. In this way, the earth acts like a sponge. If you dig a very deep hole in the earth, you can find this water. A well is a very deep hole dug in the ground to get water. A bucket, just like the one in the picture, is used to get water from a well.

Water and Ice

When water gets cold enough, it freezes to become ice. If you want something to stay frozen, you have to keep it cold. That's why ice cream and Popsicles are kept in a freezer. Water freezes outside, too. Lakes and rivers freeze when they get cold enough. Ocean water doesn't freeze because it is salty. Snow is frozen drops of rain. Snow falls from clouds the same way rain does. Can you guess what happens if you heat up a snowdrop?

All Living Things Need to Drink

Whenever you are thirsty, you have a drink. All animals need to drink from time to time. Plants also need water. They can get it from the soil through their roots. If the earth didn't hold on to water, no plants or animals—not even people—could live on the earth. All living things need water to live.

Rivers and streams flow into lakes and fill them up with water. The water that fills up rivers and streams comes from rain and melted snow.

THE AIR AROUND THE EARTH

A Blanket of Air

All people, animals, and even plants need air to live. If there wasn't any air on the earth, everything would die. A thick blanket of air covers the whole earth. No matter where you are, you can breathe because of this air. This special blanket of air around the earth is called the **atmosphere**. It covers every part of the earth, even the oceans and seas.

A Helicopter

When you turn a screw with a screwdriver, the screw goes farther and farther into the wood. Air is not as hard as wood. But you can screw things into air in the same way you can with a screwdriver. This helicopter stays up in the air by turning its blades very fast. In the same way that the screwdriver cuts into wood, the helicopter cuts into the air.

Air Can Burn

When you pedal fast on your bike, you can feel the air rushing against your face. The faster you go, the more you feel the wind. Suppose you could peddle your bicycle as fast as a rocket flies. You would be going so fast that the wind would burn your skin. When a rocket travels very fast, it can catch fire. This is because the air hitting the rocket is going so fast. To protect rockets and shuttles from catching fire, they are built with a special fireproof covering.

Protected by Air

Sometimes the sun is so strong that it can give you sunburn. But even on a very hot day, not all the sun's heat reaches the earth. This is because the atmosphere around the earth protects it from the sun's rays. This thick blanket of air keeps the sun from making the earth too hot. The atmosphere also protects the earth at night. It keeps the earth from getting too cold. What can people do to protect themselves from the bright sun?

Air Makes Blue Skies

The sun gives us light. Light from the sun looks white. But light is really made up of different colors—blue, yellow, green, and red. When light from the sun comes to earth, the blue color in light is reflected by little pieces of dust and tiny drops of water. In the large sky, there are thousands of tiny bits of dust and water. Each piece reflects a tiny bit of blue light and together they all make the sky look blue.

Air Makes the Wind

The air around the earth is never still. If you go outside you can see this. Your hat will blow off your head. Or leaves will fly. This moving air is called **wind**. Wind blows over the earth. It blows at sea, in the countryside, and in cities and towns. How hard the wind blows and where it blows changes with the weather.

*You can't hold air in your hand. You can't drink air from a glass. You can't see air because it is a **gas**.*

THE MANY DIFFERENT ANIMALS

Animals in the Hot Desert

The land is very dry in the hot desert. It almost never rains and there is little water. Only a few plants grow. The sun is very hot. Some desert animals hide under rocks to keep out of the heat. Other small desert animals bury themselves in the sand to stay cool. The animal in this picture is a dromedary. It is accustomed to life in the hot desert. It can live without water for 80 days. All desert animals can live in very hot weather and with little water.

Animals in the Thick Forest

Deep in the forests of Africa and South America, it is very hot and **humid**. It rains very often. All the trees and plants grow so thickly that everything is green. Many different animals live in forests. Monkeys swing from branch to branch. Butterflies and birds fly between the flowers. Insects, bats, bears, frogs, and snakes also live together in forests.

Animals in the Deep Ocean

There are many oceans and seas on the earth. Some are so big that it takes many days to cross them by ship. Some have waves that are so rough that no one can swim in them. Some are very, very deep. They are so deep that it is difficult for anyone to go down to the bottom— even in the best submarine! But many fish and other creatures live in oceans and seas. Whales, crabs, starfish, sharks, and other sea animals are all at home there.

ON THE EARTH

Animals at the North and South Pole

In countries close to the North Pole, it is very cold. It is so cold that trees cannot grow. In such places, ice covers the land and sea all year round. But even in these very cold lands, some animals can live. The white polar bear has thick fur that protects it from icy weather. On the other side of the earth is the South Pole. It also is very cold. Penguins, seals, and many different birds that are accustomed to cold weather live together at the South Pole.

Animals in the High Mountains

On the parts of the earth where there are many mountains, the ground is very rocky and rough. Some mountains are much too rough for cars to travel on. Only mountain climbers can climb them with special equipment. But for the animals of the mountains, climbing is no problem. Mountain goats like the one in the picture jump from rock to rock and never fall. Snakes, rabbits, deer, and many birds also live in these high hills.

Animals in Green Fields

All parts of the earth are different. If you drive to the countryside, you will see how different the earth can be—even near your home! You may see areas with lots of trees. You may see fields where sheep and cows graze. You may see farms with chickens and geese. Or you may see mountains and hills. Animals live on every type of land on the earth. The kinds of animals you see will depend on where you are.

Look back at the big picture. Did you see an owl, a lion, a porcupine, and a zebra? In what part of the earth do you think these animals live?

EXPLORERS OF THE EARTH

Studying the Oceans

Scientists are studying life in the oceans around the world. They measure the movement of the ocean and the movement of the rocks at the bottom of the sea. They catch underwater animals and pick underwater plants. Then they study what they have gathered. They learn how oceans were formed, why they change, and how sea creatures live. Scientists who study the oceans are called oceanographers.

Discovering the History of the Earth

A geologist studies rocks to learn about the history of the earth. Some rocks come from deep inside the earth. Others are from the earth's crust. Some rocks are changed by strong winds. Some are changed by the ocean washing over them. Geologists study rocks to learn about how the earth was made. They also try to discover exactly how old the earth is. Most geologists think it is about four and a half billion years old!

Exploring in Caves

Spelunkers are scientists who study caves. A cave is like a large empty room in the earth's crust. Some caves are formed by water that flows under the earth. Some caves are long and thin, like underground tunnels. Others are very small. Most caves have an opening on the earth's surface. But sometimes the opening is hard to find. Some caves are so dark inside that you can get lost. So if you ever go into a cave, watch out!

Learning About Plants

Thousands of plants grow in all parts of the world. Some grow on mountains, some in forests, some in cities, and some in the sea. Some plants have beautiful flowers. Some plants are always green. Others are never green. Some plants grow as big as a house. Some are so tiny that they can hardly be seen. Scientists who study plants are called botanists. They know how and where plants grow. They also know many other things about plants.

Learning About Animals

Zoologists are scientists who study animals. They examine all the different kinds of animals on the earth to learn how they are different. They look at fur, feathers, scales, tails, and many other things. They try to understand why animals live where they live and behave as they do. They film them when they fight, when they chase each other, and when they eat. They record their screams, cries, and other sounds to help understand them.

Learning How People Live

In all the countries of the world, people live in many different ways. People live in different kinds of houses. They eat different foods. They speak different languages. They wear different clothes and have different customs. By observing the way people of different countries live, we can better understand all people. Scientists who study the way people live and behave are called anthropologists.

What on the earth would you like to study most? If you studied birds, you would be an ornithologist. If you studied butterflies, you would be a lepidopterist.

THE MOON AND THE EARTH

Everything Is Lighter on the Moon

Like the earth, the moon has gravity that pulls and holds everything to it. But the moon has very little gravity. This is because the moon is much smaller than the earth. When astronauts walk on the moon, they feel very light. They bounce around the moon as if they weighed almost nothing. Astronauts wear special shoes to make it easier for them to walk on the moon. These shoes are very heavy and hold the astronauts down on the ground.

No Air and No Wind

The earth's gravity is so strong that it can hold its own blanket of air around it. But there is no air on the moon because the moon's gravity cannot hold it. Without air the moon has no wind either. If an astronaut dropped a feather on the moon, there would be no wind to blow it around. If an astronaut dropped a hammer and a feather together, they would both fall to the ground at the same speed. This is because there is no air or wind to hold the feather up.

A Moon Car

In the engine of a car on the earth, lighted gasoline and air mix together to make a tiny explosion. Lots of these explosions turn the car's motor so it will run. For driving on the moon, scientists had to make a car that would not need air. The kind of car they made was an electric car like the one shown in the picture. The motor of the electric car works with very large batteries.

ARE DIFFERENT

The Moon's Dry Ground

There are no rivers or lakes on the moon. It never rains and it never will. This is because there is no air. (Do you remember where rain comes from?) There is no water anywhere on the moon. The footprints left by the astronauts have not been washed or blown away by rain or wind. These footprints will stay on the dry surface of the moon for thousands and thousands of years.

Rocks Crash into the Moon

The moon's surface is covered with shallow holes, like the ones in this picture. These are called **craters**. Craters are made when the thousands of rocks that travel in space crash into the moon. Because the moon has no atmosphere to protect it, there is nothing to stop these rocks from hitting the moon. Some of these rocks are big. Some are small. Some of the holes the rocks make are as small as your hand. Others are as big as a country.

Looking Down at the Earth

The first time the earth was ever seen from very far away was in 1969. That was when two American astronauts first walked on the moon. They looked down from space and saw the small earth many, many miles away. The earth looked very different when it was seen from the moon. The astronauts saw a small blue marble swirled with brown and green and blue and white. How strange that this was the amazing earth!

Because there is no air on the moon, there is no oxygen for people to breathe. People, animals, and plants could not live on the moon. But the earth is perfect for all of them!

GLOSSARY

ATMOSPHERE   The thick blanket of air that covers and protects the earth.

CONTINENTS   Very large areas of land on the earth. *The United States is part of the* continent *of North America.*

CRATERS   Shallow holes with a raised rim often seen on the moon.

CRUST   The solid, rocky, outer part of the earth.

EARTHQUAKE   A sudden shaking and cracking of the earth's crust. *Sometimes an* earthquake *will leave big cracks in the earth's crust.*

EVAPORATION   The process by which a liquid is changed to a gas. The sun evaporates liquid water, changing it to water vapor (gas).

FLOW   To move or run easily. *Rivers* flow *down mountains quickly.*

GAS   Something that is not a solid and not a liquid. *Steam from a kettle is a* gas.

GLACIERS   Very big pieces of ice that move on the sea or on land. Some of these pieces are as big as islands.

GLOBE   A round model that shows what the earth looks like.

GRAVITY   The force that holds everything on the earth to the ground.

HUMID   Filled with water. *Before a rainstorm, the air is hot and* humid.

ICEBERGS   Very big pieces of ice that float in the sea. Some of these pieces of ice are as big as islands.

INVISIBLE   Something that cannot be seen.

LAVA   Very hot, liquid rock that sprays out of the earth during a volcano.

LIQUID   Anything that pours easily. *Water is a* liquid.

PLAINS   Large, flat areas of land.

REVOLVES   To move in a path around a central point. *The earth* revolves *around the sun.*

ROTATE   To turn or spin. *The earth and a toy top both* rotate *in the same way.*

SATELLITE   A smaller object that revolves around a larger one in space.

SURFACE   The crust of the earth and moon; the ground. *The earth's* surface *is covered with land and water.*

VOLCANO   A very large cone of rock built from hot liquid rock that flows or explodes out of the earth's crust.

WIND   Moving air that blows in every direction. *The weather depends on the way the* wind *blows.*

INDEX